KU-453-235

ENERGY ALTERNATIVES

Robert Snedden

www.heinemann.co.uk/library

To order:
☎ Phone 44 (0) 1865 888112
🖹 Send a fax to 44 (0) 1865 314091
🖥 Visit the Heinemann bookshop at www.heinemann.co.uk/library to browse our catalogue and order online.

First published in Great Britain by Heinemann Library,
Halley Court, Jordan Hill, Oxford OX2 8EJ,
part of Harcourt Education.
Heinemann is a registered trademark of Harcourt Education Ltd.

Editorial: Clare Lewis
Design: David Poole and Damco Solutions Ltd
Illustrations: Jeff Edwards
Picture Research: Maria Joannou
Production: Helen McCreath

Originated by Chroma Graphics
Printed and bound in WKT Company Ltd in China

10 digit ISBN 0 431 11771 3
10 09 08 07 06

13 digit ISBN 978 0 431 11771 3
10 9 8 7 6 5 4 3 2 1

British Library Cataloguing in Publication Data
Snedden, Robert
Energy Alternatives – 2nd Ed – (Essential Energy)
333.7'94
A full catalogue record for this book is available from the British Library.

Acknowledgements
The publishers would like to thank the following for permission to reproduce photographs:
Camera Press: Pg.24; Corbis: Pg.5, Pg.6, Pg.26, Pg.28, Pg.32, Pg.36, Pg.38, Pg.41; Empics: Pg.23; Environmental Images: Pg.12, Pg.15, Pg.19, Pg.27, Pg.29, Pg.31; Ginny Stroud Lewis: Pg.21; Popperfoto: Pg.13, Pg.33, Pg.42; Science Photo Library: Pg.4, Pg.7, Pg.16, Pg.17, Pg.20, Pg.25, Pg.30, Pg.39, Pg.40; South American Pictures: Pg.34; Still Pictures: Pg.35; United States Environmental Protection Agency: Pg.11.

Cover photograph of solar panels in the desert, reproduced with permission of Photolibrary.com/Phototake Inc..

The publishers would like to thank Helen Lloyd for her assistance in the preparation of this book.

Every effort has been made to contact copyright holders of any material reproduced in this book. Any omissions will be rectified in subsequent printings if notice is given to the publishers.

The paper used to print this book comes from sustainable resources.

CONTENTS

Any words appearing in the text in bold, **like this** are explained in the glossary.

TODAY'S QUESTIONS, TOMORROW'S ANSWERS?

While the world had a plentiful supply of **fossil fuels** there seemed to be little need to look for alternatives. Many people thought that alternative energy technologies were something that could be worked out and developed by future generations. Now there is a growing realization that the future is upon us and that it is this generation that must come up with the solutions.

Oil crisis

In 1973 the world was shaken when the Organization of Petroleum Exporting Countries (**OPEC**) quadrupled the price of oil. Europe, the United States, and most of the rest of the world were faced with an energy crisis. Thoughts turned towards alternative energy sources. The US Congress established the Solar Energy Research Institute (SERI) and breakthroughs were made in developing **solar-energy** technology. President Jimmy Carter even installed a water-heating solar-energy panel at the White House.

However, the energy crisis passed as OPEC members increased oil production and fuel supplies began to flow again. As oil prices fell, so too did interest in energy conservation and alternative energy. In 1981, for example, the US government cut SERI's funding almost by half, as once again alternative energy was sidelined in favour of **nuclear energy** and fossil fuel sources. In 2000, energy hit the headlines again as high fuel prices led to protests across Europe.

■ A coal-fired power station in Germany. Pollution problems and shrinking resources mean alternatives have to be found.

4

Looking for alternatives

Today we are perhaps more aware of the need to find an alternative to fossil fuels, not only because they are a dwindling resource, but also because of the environmental consequences of their use, such as smog, **acid rain**, **global warming**, and oil spills. Nuclear power, once seen as an answer to our energy problems, presents its own difficulties and hazards. The disposal of hazardous nuclear waste and the danger of terrible accidents such as that at Chernobyl in 1986 has led many to question the nuclear solution.

There can be no doubt that we need to cut down on the use of fossil fuels, and there are alternatives. Solar power has already been mentioned. Wind power has been used for centuries to drive windmills. Today it can be harnessed more efficiently to generate electricity using wind **turbines**. Ocean waves and tides can be used to drive **generators** to produce electricity. Animal and plant wastes can be processed to produce **natural gas**. This **biomass** energy is widely used in many parts of the world. **Geothermal energy** comes from the hot rock inside the Earth. In places such as Iceland and New Zealand it is used to generate electricity and to heat buildings. **Hydroelectricity**, once thought to be a clean way of producing power, is now frowned upon by many because of the disastrous effects dam building can have on the environment.

But which, if any, of these alternatives to fossil fuels is the best? What are the drawbacks involved in making the switch? What lies in the future for energy?

■ An erupting geyser is evidence of the geothermal energy beneath the Earth's surface.

WHY DO WE NEED ENERGY?

We can't see energy directly, but we can see what it can do. The warmth on your face on a summer's day is caused by energy radiating out from the Sun through 150 million kilometres (93 million miles) of space. But you can't see that heat heading towards you. Every time you throw a ball, energy stored in chemicals in your arm muscles becomes the energy of movement in the ball. But you can't see that change taking place. If you took a photograph of the ball as it flew through the air it would look no different from a ball on the ground. You can't see the energy that makes it move.

Work and energy

Energy makes things happen. Without energy everything would come to a standstill. Science defines energy as the ability to do work. Work is what happens as a result of transferring energy from one place to another. When you threw that ball you were doing work!

Energy cannot be created or destroyed, but it can be converted into different forms. The energy stored in your muscles is an example of **chemical energy** and the energy of movement that you gave the ball is called **kinetic energy**. When the ball hits the ground, this energy will become sound and **heat energy**.

■ As the ball is thrown the chemical energy in the body's muscles is turned into the kinetic energy of the ball.

Energy resources

Most of our energy, apart from **nuclear** and **geothermal energy**, comes from the Sun. Inside the Sun, under enormous pressures and temperatures, hydrogen **atoms** join together and become helium. This process is called **nuclear fusion** and it releases large amounts of energy that radiate out into space to reach the Earth as heat and light. Plants convert this **solar energy** into **chemical energy**, and animals eat plants to obtain their stored chemical energy.

The energy stored in **fossil fuels** also came from the Sun. Fossil fuels are the remains of ancient plants and animals that lived millions of years ago. After the plants and animals died, they were slowly buried deep underground where, after millions of years, they eventually turned into coal and **petroleum**. When we burn fossil fuels today we are releasing stored energy from the Sun.

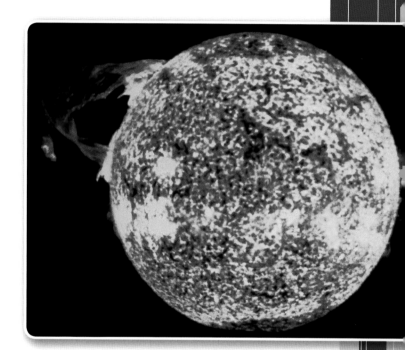

■ The Sun – ultimate source of almost all of the energy we use

Renewable energy

Fossil fuels supply most of our energy needs. However, these are nonrenewable sources of energy. This means that the amount of fossil fuel available is limited and one day we will have used it all up. Scientists are trying to find renewable sources of energy that won't run out and can be used in place of fossil fuels, and there are several that look promising. So far, however, none seem to be as useful or as convenient to use as fossil fuels. Our dependence on fossil fuels was demonstrated forcefully in a wave of protests against fuel taxes in the summer of 2000. Britain almost came to a standstill when the protesters blocked the movement of fuel tankers.

ENERGY EFFICIENCY

Before looking at alternative sources of energy, it is useful to see how we are making use of the energy we have available at present. One way of improving the energy problem is to use the energy sources we have more efficiently and cut down on waste.

Measuring efficiency

There are several ways to measure how efficiently we use our energy resources. One way is to compare the amount of energy being used with the work it is being used to do. For example, we can ask how many kilometres a car will travel (the work) on a litre of petrol (the energy). We can also compare the energy actually used to do something with the theoretical minimum needed under ideal conditions. We can find out if our machines are using energy efficiently, or if a change in design would lead to greater efficiency.

0–1.5
1.5–3.0
3.0–4.5
4.5–6.0
> 6.0

■ Primary energy consumption across the world expressed as the equivalent of tonnes of oil per person.

Energy use

We use a lot of energy to heat our homes and places of work in winter and to cool them in summer. We use electricity to light our towns and cities, and to operate our televisions, radios, computers, refrigerators, washing machines, and any number of gadgets. Most of this electricity is produced by burning **fossil fuels**, which are a convenient source of energy, but are also polluting and nonrenewable.

Fossil fuel energy powers our cars and other vehicles. Today's cars are much more efficient than they were 20 years ago and will travel a lot further on a tank of petrol. However, there are now many more cars on the road and they are being used much more frequently.

Factories use energy to make all the goods we, as **consumers**, demand, including preparing and packaging the food we eat, the clothes we wear, the furniture in our homes, the books we read, and the games we play, and indeed everything that money can buy.

Plastics are made from oil and so use up fossil fuels both physically and in the energy used for their manufacture. Many plastic products are designed to be used once and then discarded.

ENERGY CONSUMPTION

Four sets of factors determine how much energy is used in a society:

Population and geography: A big country with a cold climate and a lot of people will tend to consume more energy than a small country where the weather is fine.

Economic factors: Although there is no direct relationship between national income and energy use, higher-income countries with more industry do use more energy than poorer, less-industrialized countries.

Technological factors: These determine how efficiently machines use energy.

Lifestyles: Our lifestyle includes a variety of energy-related factors. For example, we can choose whether or not to live in smaller houses, buy more efficient cars, **recycle** as much as possible and use public transport.

HOME ECONOMICS

As home-buyers become aware of the costs of energy and the damage done to the environment through pollution and **global warming**, energy efficiency is becoming a strong selling point for houses. After all, energy efficiency does not just save the environment, it saves money, too.

There are many things we can all do to save energy. **Insulation**, in roofs and in wall cavities, makes a real difference to energy consumption. Up to 40 per cent of the heating in a home can escape through the ceiling. Double glazing is highly efficient at saving energy. Thermostatic controls on radiators and on the hot-water tank help. One simple way of saving energy would be to have radiator thermostats that cannot be put above a set temperature, say 23°C (73°F). In fact, putting on warm clothing indoors on a cold day could mean not having to turn up the thermostat.

Remembering to turn off all the lights when you leave a room will save electricity. Replacing ordinary light bulbs with energy-saving bulbs, sometimes called compact fluorescent lights, will save more energy, as these bulbs use only about a quarter of the energy of normal light bulbs and last around eight times longer. Don't leave radios, televisions, or computers switched on if no one is using them.

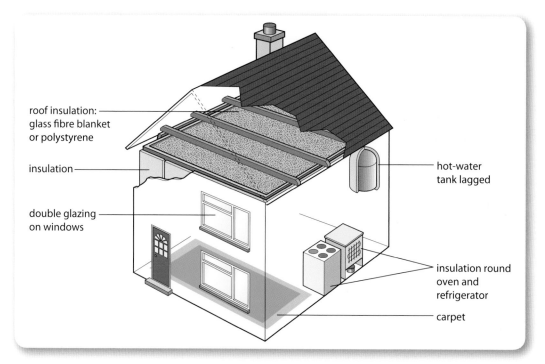

roof insulation: glass fibre blanket or polystyrene

insulation

double glazing on windows

hot-water tank lagged

insulation round oven and refrigerator

carpet

■ Effective insulation can have a dramatic effect on energy costs.

Recycle and save

Everyone should recycle newspapers because paper made from recycled paper uses about one third less energy than paper made from raw materials. Glass bottles should be recycled because glass made from recycled glass also uses about one third less energy than glass made from raw materials. Recycling steel and aluminium cans and aluminium foil is very energy efficient. It takes 90 per cent less energy to make an aluminium can from recycled materials than it does to make one from scratch using raw materials.

ENERGY STAR

The Energy Star programme has been set up jointly by the United States Environmental Protection Agency and the Department of Energy to promote the use of energy-efficient products. Products are awarded an Energy Star label if they meet or exceed the minimum standards set by the programme. There are well over 3,000 Energy Star products, ranging from light bulbs that burn brighter for longer to washing machines that use up to 60 per cent less energy than average appliances. The European Union is also keen on strengthening the use of energy-efficiency labelling schemes for commercial equipment and for household appliances. It recommends setting minimum efficiency standards for appliances such as water heaters, air conditioners, dishwashers, electric motors, pumps, and commercial refrigeration equipment.

Money Isn't All You're Saving

■ The energy star on packaging assures consumers that they are buying an energy efficient product.

TRANSPORT TECHNOLOGY

There are more cars and other vehicles on our roads than there have ever been before and the numbers show no signs of decreasing. Like so many other aspects of alternative energy, the enthusiasm for developing transport alternatives seems to rise and fall with the oil prices. Falling oil prices appear to encourage people to drive around in four-wheel drive vehicles that will never go near a mountain road and are more like fashion accessories than an efficient way to get around town. So what alternative forms of transport are on offer, now and in the future, to conserve energy?

Cutting down on carbon dioxide

In industrialized countries, such as those of the European Union and North America, transportation accounts for around 30 per cent of energy usage and over 80 per cent of carbon dioxide emissions. This is a serious issue because carbon dioxide is a **greenhouse gas** and strongly believed by many to be contributing to the overall warming of the Earth and consequent changes in the global climate.

It is obvious that there are savings to be made. To cut down on petrol consumption we could all walk or cycle a little more rather than going everywhere by car. For longer journeys we might think about using the bus or train instead. In many places, however, public transport is poor and efforts will have to be made to improve standards if car drivers are to be persuaded to change over.

■ Cars consume vast quantities of petrol, and vehicle exhaust is a major source of pollution.

Petroleum substitutes

Petrol and other **petroleum**-based fuels supply nearly all the energy for the engines that power the world's transportation systems. Fuel conservation is necessary, not only because of the threat of a serious fuel shortage, but also because of the high cost of pollution, particularly from car exhausts.

More than half the energy used for transportation in the industrialized nations is consumed by cars. Governments can try to encourage car manufacturers to produce smaller, lighter cars, that are more fuel efficient and so cover a greater distance on a tank of petrol. Eventually, however, we will need to find substitutes for petroleum fuels. Already there are companies producing **synthetic** liquid fuels from coal, **natural gas**, **biomass**, oil shale, and bituminous sands (sands containing bitumen, a substance from which oil can be obtained). In Brazil, **ethanol**, also called ethyl alcohol, is made from sugar-cane pulp.

■ One of the competitors in the 1996 World Solar Challenge

SUN RACERS

The World Solar Challenge is held every two years. For the 2005 race 30 solar-powered cars lined up to race 3,000 kilometres across Australia from Darwin to Adelaide. An important aspect of the Solar Challenge is to demonstrate how alternative energy sources can effectively provide a more environmentally friendly form of transport. The best cars have average speeds of more than 100 kilometres (62 miles) per hour.

BATTERIES NOT INCLUDED

Another way of cutting down on fossil fuel consumption could be to use electric motors to power vehicles. At one point battery-powered cars were seen as the answer to vehicle pollution and fuel shortages. Regulations in California, New York, and Massachusetts even compelled the United States' seven largest car manufacturers to ensure that a minimum of two per cent of their 1998-model vehicles ran on electricity. However, electric cars have not proved popular.

Against electric

Several factors work against electric cars. They can cost £30,000, or more, and on average can only cover about 100 kilometres (62 miles) before a recharge, compared to the four or five times greater distance covered by a car using a full tank of petrol. There are also few places along the road where you can plug in your recharger. If you can plug it in, it will take four to eight hours to recharge the electric vehicle's battery, compared with the five minutes or so it takes to refill a petrol tank.

Hybrids

One way to get around some of the problems posed by electric cars is to combine electricity with **internal combustion engines** in what are known as **hybrid** vehicles. Hybrids use small diesel engines or gas **turbines** that act as on-board **generators** to recharge the batteries, thus extending the vehicle's range. The hybrid uses a nickel-metal-hydride battery pack designed specifically for use in hybrid vehicles.

General Motors has produced a hybrid electric vehicle that uses a 137-horsepower electric motor for propulsion and a small gas turbine acting as a generator to keep the nickel-metal-hydride battery pack charged. This hybrid should have a range of nearly 600 kilometres (370 miles) and has a top speed of 130 kilometres (80 miles) per hour. It is also much less polluting than a car using a conventional internal combustion engine.

ELECTRIC VEHICLES

The first mass-produced electric vehicle was General Motors' EV1. Two years after it came on the market at the end of 1996, just over 500 had been sold. However, sales of hybrid cars have taken off, prompted by high fuel prices. In 2004, 80,000 hybrid cars were sold in the United States (around 0.5% of total car sales). This figure is expected to rise to around 500,000 by 2011.

Computer controlled

Production costs remain one of the greatest potential problems for electric vehicles and hybrids. Hybrids need more sophisticated control systems than ordinary cars. A hybrid's fuel efficiency can be cut dramatically under real driving conditions. Air conditioners, windscreen wipers, heaters, defoggers, defrosters, and headlights all drain power from the battery. Bad weather and the stop-go driving conditions encountered in towns and cities can lower the fuel economy even more.

With new computer systems, the hybrid vehicles would be able to adjust to the weather, traffic, and a driver's habits. Sophisticated control systems would, for example, adapt to the driver, learning how hard they accelerate and how hard they brake. Hybrids are well-suited for such techniques because, unlike conventional vehicles which waste energy when braking, they can store energy for later use. They use their internal combustion engines only as a way to store charge in the batteries, not to provide a driving force. Electrical current is released to the electric motor by the control system as it is needed.

Some environmentalists remain optimistic about electric cars. Nickel-metal-hydride batteries, currently being developed, will double the distance that could be covered by the lead acid batteries used in the EV1. However, many people see new **fuel-cell** powered vehicles as far more promising.

■ An electric car recharges its battery. Some hybrid cars, known as parallel hybrids, can use either an internal combustion engine or an electric motor to drive the car.

FUEL CELLS

Fuel cells appear to be the ideal solution to many of our energy problems. They generate electricity by combining hydrogen and oxygen, producing water as a harmless "waste" product. Unlike a battery, the reacting chemicals are not stored inside the cell but supplied from outside, and the waste products are removed. Car manufacturers are currently investing large sums of money in the development of fuel cells. Many energy experts believe hydrogen gas could one day become an environmentally friendly replacement for **fossil fuels**.

■ A fuel cell inside Europe's first hydrogen-powered taxi.

Hydrogen sources

The biggest problem in developing fuel cells lies in obtaining a source of hydrogen. One way might be to split water by **electrolysis** into hydrogen and oxygen but this requires energy. The alternative involves taking hydrogen from hydrocarbon **molecules** of the sort found in fossil fuels. A piece of equipment, called a reformer, performs this task in prototype fuel-cell powered vehicles. However, the chemical processes involved produce carbon dioxide, a **greenhouse gas**, as a by-product.

The best results (that is the greatest amount of hydrogen that can be produced for the least amount of carbon dioxide), comes from processing methane, the biggest constituent of **natural gas**. Every methane molecule is made up of one carbon and four hydrogen **atoms** – the greatest ratio of hydrogen to carbon that is possible. Natural gas is also cheap and easy to reform into hydrogen and carbon dioxide. It is believed that a car running on a fuel cell that uses methane to obtain its hydrogen would be no more expensive to run than a car using unleaded petrol. Of course, natural gas is itself a fossil fuel, and so in limited supply, although it can be produced from biological wastes.

Another problem with natural gas is that it takes up a lot of space, even when compressed or liquefied. This could mean that, in the short term, natural gas would only be used in those vehicles with the capacity to carry a sufficient amount of fuel, such as trucks and buses.

One possible solution is to extract the hydrogen in large reformers at filling stations and then store it on board vehicles in solids known as metal hydrides. A United States firm called Energy Conversion Devices unveiled a device that can soak up hydrogen so well that a tank of hydride can deliver as much energy as a similarly-sized tank of petrol. The alternative, of course, is to strap a giant gas bag to the roof of your car!

■ Apollo 11 lifts off on its way to the Moon in 1969. Fuel cells provided the electrical power for the spacecraft.

Hydrogen and algae

Scientists in the US have recently discovered an alga (a type of simple plant) that produces hydrogen. The researchers first grow the alga under normal conditions, allowing the **micro-organisms** to collect sunlight and make carbohydrates through **photosynthesis**. When enough energy has been stored chemically in this way, the alga is transferred into bottles from which all sulphur (a chemical that is essential for photosynthesis) has been removed.

By turning off the alga's ability to photosynthesize, the scientists stop it from producing oxygen and force it to switch to another way of generating energy that produces hydrogen as a by-product. After up to four days of generating hydrogen, the alga has used up its stored fuel and must be allowed to return to photosynthesis. Then, two or three days later, it can be tapped for hydrogen once more.

COMBINED HEAT AND POWER

Industrial nations such as Britain, France, and the United States discard as much energy in the form of waste heat from electricity production as they obtain from **natural gas**. Combined heat and power, or CHP, makes efficient use of fuels by using the waste heat from electricity generation to heat homes and factories close to the power station, or in industry. CHP is not a new idea. In fact, the first power plant built by Thomas Edison in 1881 was a CHP plant.

The electricity output from a CHP plant is lower than from a conventional station, but this is more than offset by the energy savings from using the waste heat effectively. A typical CHP plant may convert 80 per cent of the original fuel energy into a mix of electricity and useful heat, whereas a conventional power station rarely ever achieves a 40 per cent conversion rate.

Hot water from the CHP station is pumped through **insulated** pipes into the heating systems of buildings nearby. The buildings being heated are taking the place of the conventional power station's cooling towers. The low cost of the heat makes this the cheapest method available of providing warmth for towns and cities. About 50 per cent of buildings in Denmark and Finland are heated from CHP plants, which provide a third of those countries' electricity.

The European Union has urged member states to double their output from CHP plants as part of a drive to cut emissions of **greenhouse gases**. It is possible that within 10 years or so, CHPs and small gas **turbines** will be generating as much as 30 to 40 per cent of Europe's power.

CHP and biofuel

In Scandinavia, CHPs have been made even more energy efficient and environmentally friendly. A Swedish company has built a **biofuel** pellet manufacturing facility at its CHP plant. The company can produce an easily transportable, high-energy biofuel using **heat energy** from the CHP plant. The plant has an output of approximately 63 megawatts of heat and 35 megawatts of electricity. When heat requirements are high in winter only electricity and heat are produced. When there is heat to spare the pellet factory is started up. In this way, the steam flow in the CHP unit is kept at a constant and even level. As a result, the electrical efficiency of the turbine can be kept high, because

■ This power station in Sweden generates energy by burning waste materials rather than fossil fuels.

it falls with any drop in the steam flow. The additional electrical production arising from this greater efficiency can be as much as 2.5 megawatts.

The bulk of the pellets produced are sold to existing CHP plants as a substitute for coal. Pellets will also be sold to small heating plants and to domestic users. Compared with wood, pellets are much easier for the **consumer** to store and handle.

MICRO CHPS

Small-scale CHP plants, based on **internal combustion engines** burning liquid **petroleum** gas or **natural gas**, can be used to provide energy for office blocks, hospitals, and small groups of houses. These "micro-CHPs" typically have outputs of around 15 kilowatts of electricity and 25 kilowatts of heat. A CHP unit now provides heat and light to the European Parliament building in Brussels.

SOLAR ENERGY

It is the Sun's energy that ultimately powers practically all life on Earth and keeps the planet warm enough for that life to exist. Until recently, however, we have lacked the means to tap this energy and put it to practical use.

Energy in abundance

Only about one two-billionth part of the Sun's energy output reaches the Earth. Yet even that tiny fraction would supply all the world's energy needs if we could only find the means of capturing it. Every day, the Sun generates more energy than the Earth's six billion people use in about 30 years.

Solar thermal collectors

One method of capturing **solar energy** involves using solar thermal collectors. These are the heat-absorbing black solar panels seen on some rooftops. Flat plate collectors absorb solar energy and change it to **heat energy**. Water circulates through the panels, where the heat energy is transferred to it. The water is then stored in tanks. Solar water heating is growing in popularity as the price of the technology falls.

■ A solar power station looks quite unlike a conventional power station. Here, photovoltaic cells stretch out across the Californian desert.

Solar thermal collectors can also be used to produce electricity. The panels use the Sun's rays to produce sufficient energy to heat water enough to turn it into steam. The steam is then used to run **turbines** to generate electricity, just as it is in a conventional power station.

Photovoltaic cells

Photovoltaic cells were invented in 1954 at AT&T's Bell Laboratories in the United States and later were used to power satellites and space vehicles. Now they provide power not only for satellites, but also provide electricity and heat water for homes and businesses around the world. Used together with other **renewable energy** sources, such as wind and water, photovoltaic cells can provide energy for entire homes – even entire communities.

Battery banks

A major problem with solar power is that, of course, the Sun does not shine at night. If we want solar electricity at night we must find some means of storing it during the day. Small machines, such as portable computers, can be powered by batteries

■ Photovoltaic cells power many calculators and all solar-powered cars. They are made of silicon and other materials, and convert the Sun's rays directly into electricity.

that are recharged in daylight using photovoltaic cells. Solar energy could also be used to create hydrogen from water for use in **fuel cells** (see page 16).

Large electric motors used to run a building's air-conditioning system or to power lifts would need large banks of batteries for operation at night or on cloudy days. When the Sun is hidden the battery bank discharges power. When the Sun shines the batteries discharge less power as more solar energy becomes available. Around midday the photovoltaic cells begin to produce more energy than is needed and start to recharge the batteries. The batteries continue to charge throughout the daylight hours. The battery bank is a critical part of the solar-powered building. Already, banks have been developed that can supply power throughout five days of overcast weather.

SOLAR DEVELOPMENTS

The day may come when our homes, school, and work places are heated by **solar energy** and most of our machinery is solar-powered. Solar energy is clean, safe, and plentiful, but it is a big step from the solar-powered pocket calculator to an entirely solar-powered office block.

Electrical engineers and other scientists are seeking ways to make cheaper and more efficient **photovoltaic cells**. One way of doing this is to develop materials that are more transparent. New **silicon** parts are being produced that do not prevent the Sun's rays from hitting the light-sensitive metal part of the cell. Smaller, more light-sensitive cells will capture more sunlight, and therefore provide more energy.

Solar logos

The solar power industry is not only working on ways of improving its technology, but also looking at how that technology can be integrated more effectively into the structure of buildings. For example, roofing tiles or shingles can now be replaced by an array of solar cells. Designers can blend translucent panels into office buildings, so that many of the modern glass and steel skyscrapers in our cities could have large solar-power producing panels fitted instead of the glass. European designers are even manufacturing solar panels in different colours and shapes. As a result, a building's power source could be a design element, perhaps with a company name or logo, picked out in coloured solar panels.

A "MILLION SOLAR ROOFS"

In 1997, President Bill Clinton announced the "Million Solar Roofs" campaign in the United States. By 2010 the US government hopes to have solar energy systems installed on one million buildings throughout the United States and, in the process, create 70,000 new jobs. The US Department of Energy expects the solar energy market to exceed $1.5 billion (£2.25 billion) worldwide within the next few years.

Off the grid

While solar power is mostly used to augment or back up conventional sources of power, there are already about 20,000 homes across the United States that are "off the grid" (not drawing power from local utility companies) and totally reliant on solar power. The reason why more don't follow suit is that solar power equipment costs around three to five times as much as getting power from the grid. However, it may be worth it for people living in remote areas. It might also be worthwhile for rural communities in countries where the electricity supply grid is not as efficient as it is in the industrialized nations.

■ Many of the Sydney Olympic Stadium buildings utilized solar panels to generate power.

BLOWING IN THE WIND

Wind power is really solar power one step removed, as it is the energy of the Sun that powers the Earth's weather systems and makes the wind blow. People have harnessed the power of the wind for many centuries to grind grain, pump water, and sail ships. Wind **turbines** were first used to generate electricity in the 20th century and within the next few decades wind power may supply a significant part of our energy needs.

■ The energy of the wind powers this yacht.

Wind into electricity

Turning wind into electricity is fairly simple. Rotor blades, rather like aircraft propellers, are mounted on a tower in a suitably windy location. The wind spins the blades, which are linked to the shaft of an electricity **generator**. The generator then produces electricity which is carried by power lines to wherever it is needed. Wind turbines can be used singly or in groups known as "wind farms". The wind turbines used in a wind farm are usually about 60 metres (200 feet) tall. Other wind turbines can be much smaller. These are often called "wind chargers" because they are used to charge large batteries. They can provide power for homes with no other electricity supply.

Despite its apparent simplicity, wind power has not been used very much. The main reason for this is cost. It is no small undertaking to build several hundred 60-metre (200-feet) tall turbines. In the early 1980s, wind-generated electricity was up to three times more expensive than traditional **fossil fuel** generated power. By the early 1990s, new designs had cut the cost of wind power to a more competitive level.

The United States is currently the world's leading consumer of wind power. In Europe several countries are rapidly developing wind energy as they look for ways to reduce their reliance on fossil fuels and **nuclear energy**, and to cut down on pollution. Britain has relatively high average wind speeds making it a good location. In December 2003 the UK government announced 15 new offshore wind farms, which will provide enough energy for four million homes. More than one in six households should be powered by wind by 2010.

The right site

The most important factor in the effectiveness of a wind farm is its location. Most are in places where the wind is strongest, such as Wales, Scotland, and Cornwall in Britain and North Dakota and California in the United States. The biggest problem, perhaps, is that wind farms take up large areas of land. Land is valuable, especially in a small crowded country, such as Britain. However, this difficulty can be overcome if wind farms are put on land used for other purposes, such as farming.

Wind speed isn't everything. It is also vital that the wind blows steadily. If the wind blows for an hour or less a day, it will not be enough to generate power. No one is sure just how important wind power could be. One study estimated that around half of the United States' electricity needs could be met by wind farms scattered around the country's windiest areas. Even if that proves to be wildly optimistic, it would appear that wind power has enormous potential.

■ A wind farm at Altamont Pass, California.

DRAWBACKS

Although wind is a clean and renewable source of energy, wind farms are not popular with everyone. People living near wind farms complain that the turbines are noisy. Positioning them in rural areas and out at sea can block what were once beautiful views. Campaigners also complain that birds can get caught in the blades of turbines.

HYDROELECTRICITY

Hydroelectric power is generated from the **kinetic energy** of moving water, a powerful and **renewable energy** source. Currently about four per cent of the world's energy needs are generated in this way. Some estimates suggest that around 20 per cent of our energy requirements could be met if all suitable sites were exploited. In common with many other renewable energy sources, hydroelectricity is a clean source of power and does not produce air pollution.

Hydro-history

The power of running water was first harnessed using water wheels placed in rivers where the currents caught their large blades and made them spin. The Romans used water wheels to move grindstones to mill their grain. In the 17th and 18th centuries, rivers and streams were dammed and redirected throughout Europe. People used water energy for grinding wheat and other cereals, to pump water from wells, and to drive spinning wheels and other equipment in textile production.

Hydroelectric dams

At the end of the 19th century a new way of using water appeared – the hydroelectric dam. It was far more efficient in capturing the energy of rushing water than water wheels. The most common form of hydroelectric power involves building dams on rivers to create large reservoirs of water. The water can then be released from the reservoirs and directed through concrete troughs (called sluices) and pipes to **turbines**, making them spin. The turbines are connected to electricity **generators**.

■ Hydroelectricity is a renewable source of energy but large dams look unsightly.

Hydropower has the benefit of being inexpensive, once the huge initial costs of constructing the dam and power station have been taken care of. The taller a dam, the more energy it can produce. This is because the higher the water, the greater its **potential energy**. More than one hundred dams around the world stand over 150 metres (490 feet) tall. The highest in the world is the Rogun Dam in Russia at 335 metres (1165 feet).

Mountainous countries such as Norway, the United States, and Canada are best placed to make use of hydroelectric power. There are more than 2,000 hydroelectric power stations in the United States and most of the rivers that could be used for hydroelectricity have been dammed. Spain and Italy get over a third of their electricity from hydroelectric power. Canada gets two thirds of its electricity from this source and exports a great deal of it to the energy-hungry United States.

FALLING FROM FAVOUR

In recent years hydroelectricity has been viewed by many as environmentally damaging. Damming rivers can change the **ecology** of a region as whole areas are flooded. The water below a dam is often colder than it would be normally, which can have an effect on fish stocks. The change in the level of water can affect the plants that grow along the riverbanks. People, too, are often displaced when river valleys are flooded. Building of the Three Gorges Dam in China has forced more than 100,000 people to move. Hydroelectric power, once seen as a clean and never-ending source of energy, has a downside just as **fossil fuels** do.

■ Despite making use of a renewable energy source, hydropower can have negative effects and many communities fight against its use.

WAVE POWER

Waves are produced by the power of the wind blowing across the sea, which means that, as the wind is powered by the Sun, wave power is really solar power twice removed. Ocean waves represent a considerable amount of energy, but it may not be easy to obtain it. Average power levels of 15 to 70 kilowatts per metre of wave front are estimated for favourable regions around the coast of Britain, which means that it would take many kilometres of wave energy machines to generate the power produced by a large **fossil fuel** station.

Ducks and buoys

Wave-power **generators** would have to be robust enough to withstand the changeable and sometimes highly adverse conditions encountered at sea. In 1974, British designer Stephen Salter developed the 'duck', a floating **boom** that got its name because the segments bob up and down like a duck as the waves pass. The nodding motion can be used to spin generators to produce electricity.

Another device, developed in Japan, uses an **oscillating** column of water to harness the wave power. A device being developed by a European consortium works on the same principles. The water columns oscillate with the movement

■ The energy carried by waves is obvious as they crash against the shore.

of the sea waves. The air displaced above the water in the columns drives an air **turbine** to generate power.

While this is still at an experimental stage, results so far indicate that the device will generate electricity more efficiently than has been achieved before from wave power. The device is a free-floating buoy, which means that it can move with the waves and so better withstand storm conditions. Devices like this could be used to supply power to remote islands and offshore oil rigs.

■ The world's first commercial wave-powered electricity generator was launched on the River Clyde in Scotland in 1995. The plant, called Osprey, was expected to generate 2 megawatts of electricity from wave power and a further 1.5 megawatts from a wind turbine. Unfortunately it failed a few weeks after launch.

OCEAN THERMAL ENERGY

The temperature of the ocean is different at different depths which offers another possible way to generate power from the oceans. **Heat energy** moves naturally from the hotter parts of the ocean to the colder parts. If it is channelled through a heat-powered engine, this thermal energy can be used to generate electricity. Ocean thermal energy conversion, as this is called, might be a good energy source for island nations in the Pacific Ocean, for example. But the technology required is expensive and many of the countries that would benefit most are poor. As yet there has been little research on the environmental impact of extracting energy from the ocean in this way, although there would seem to be little doubt that there would be an effect on ocean **ecosystems** if heat was extracted on a large scale.

TIDAL ENERGY

Tidal energy is a **renewable energy** source that is powered by the force of **gravity**. The idea of making use of the energy of the tides is not new. Tidal mills were built in Britain, France, and Spain as early as the 12th century. These early mills managed to produce the equivalent of 20 to 75 kilowatts of power, which is less than the power available in a modern car.

There are not that many places in the world where the tidal range (the difference between high and low tides) is large enough to justify exploitation of the available tidal energy. A tidal range of at least five metres (16.5 feet) is needed to make a tidal power station worthwhile.

The world's most powerful tides occur in the Bay of Fundy in Canada, where tidal ranges of up to 17 metres are quite common. Britain, France, the United States, north-west Australia, Argentina, Brazil, India, and Russia all have stretches of coastline with sufficiently large tidal ranges. The total capacity of all potential tidal-power sites in the world has been estimated to be about one billion kilowatts. The world's first tidal power station, in France at La Rance in Brittany, can produce enough power to provide for the needs of around 300,000 people.

Tidal technology

The ocean can be used to generate power in several ways. For example, a dam could be built across a cove or an estuary with a large tidal range. The dam would be composed of a powerhouse, a sluiceway section, and a solid embankment. When the tide comes in, the sluiceways are opened and the area behind the dam fills with water. At high tide the sluiceway gates are closed, and the trapped water is allowed to return to the ocean through pipes, spinning electricity-generating

■ This is the original La Rance tidal mill with its sluice gates and tidal pool.

turbines as it does so. It is possible to install turbines that can generate electricity in both directions, as the tide ebbs and as it flows. When the tide begins to turn and the sea level rises once more, the sluiceways are opened again and the dammed area fills up ready for the next cycle of electrical generation.

Time and tide

The average electric power output that can be obtained by exploiting the tides is limited by the twice daily ebb and flow of the tides. The average output of electricity from a tidal plant is less than 40 per cent of its potential generating capacity, because it is only generating

■ La Rance tidal power station in Brittany, France.

electricity half the time. In contrast, the production of power from **hydroelectric** power stations averages between 70 and 100 per cent of capacity.

Another problem is that the tides are powered by the attraction of the Moon, caused by **gravity**. The lunar cycle of 24 hours and 50 minutes means that the production of tidal energy moves in and out of step with the usual 24-hour pattern of energy consumption. In other words, the tidal power station may not be performing to capacity at the times of day when demand for power is greatest. The tidal energy must be either stored or used alongside other sources of power generation to make sure that power is there when needed.

Tidal power stations may not be able to replace conventional **fossil fuel** stations but they can work alongside them. The output from the fossil-fuelled stations can be reduced when the tidal plant begins to generate power. It can be increased again during the few hours that a tidal plant must remain idle because the flow of water is insufficient. As a result, coal and oil reserves can be conserved and pollution can be reduced.

GEOTHERMAL ENERGY

Geothermal means heat from the Earth. Resources for **geothermal energy** are widespread and include the hot water and hot rock found a few kilometres beneath the surface, and the extremely high temperatures of molten rock called magma at deeper levels. The best features of geothermal energy are that it is generally non-polluting and it is sustainable.

Geothermal pumps

Geothermal pumps make use of the fact that the top three metres or so of the Earth's surface maintains a nearly constant temperature of between 10 and 15°C (50–59°F). A geothermal heat pump system consists of a heat pump, an air delivery system and a heat exchanger, which is a system of pipes buried in the shallow ground near the building. In the winter, the heat pump removes heat from the heat exchanger and pumps it into the indoor air delivery system, warming the inside of the building. In the summer months, the process is reversed. The indoor air temperature is now greater than the shallow ground temperature and the heat pump moves heat from the indoor air into the heat exchanger. The heat removed from the indoor air can also be used to provide a free source of hot water.

Geothermal reservoirs

Heat rising from the molten magma several kilometres beneath the surface warms underground pools of water known as geothermal reservoirs. Sometimes the water is heated enough for it to boil and turn to steam. If there are openings through the rock to the surface, the hot water may seep out to form hot springs, or it may erupt out in the form of a geyser.

- Geothermal power stations can generate as much electricity as conventional power stations.

Hot water near the surface is used for heating buildings, growing plants in greenhouses, heating water at fish farms, and pasteurizing milk. Wells can tap directly into geothermal reservoirs and pump the water to the surface for use. This is called direct use of geothermal energy.

The Geysers geothermal field located in northern California, USA, is the largest source of geothermal energy in the world. It produces as much power as two large coal or nuclear power plants. Geothermal power plants can use steam directly from a reservoir to power a **turbine**.

Hot dry rocks

Hot dry rock resources occur at depths of five to eight kilometres (16 to 26 feet) everywhere beneath the Earth's surface. In areas where there is volcanic activity they will be nearer to the surface. Obtaining energy from these resources involves injecting cold water down one well, circulating it through the hot fractured rock, and then drawing off the heated water from another well. Currently, there are no commercial applications for this technology, and at present there are no means of recovering heat directly from magma. Magma is the most powerful resource of geothermal energy, but it lies at an inaccessible depth, and only reaches the Earth's surface in volcanic eruptions.

■ A volcanic eruption reveals the energy hidden within the Earth.

GEOTHERMAL FLAWS

Although geothermal energy is a clean and reliable source of power overall, it is not readily available to everyone. People either do not live near a geothermal reservoir or they lack the technology to make use of the shallow ground energy. There is a possibility that so much water could be drawn out of a reservoir that it is not able to replenish itself. In addition, water from geothermal reservoirs often contains minerals that are corrosive and polluting.

BIOMASS ENERGY

For hundreds of thousands of years, people have used wood, charcoal, and plant and animal wastes to heat and cook. These fuels, all the product of living things, are called **biomass** fuels, or simply "biomass". Today, biomass is used to generate electricity and to produce liquid fuels, such as methanol and **ethanol**, to power vehicles. Biomass fuels are an important energy source, especially in developing countries. Homes, farms, and factories produce wastes of all kinds that could be used as biomass fuel.

Bioelectric power

The biggest advances in biomass technology will probably be in the field of electricity production. Parts of the timber industry are already burning wood and paper wastes to produce steam to drive electric **generators**, but many people believe that **biogas turbines** would be more efficient. Biomass can be easily converted into methane, a fuel that can be used to power gas turbines. There are 80 countries in the developing world that produce sugar cane, a crop that generates a great deal of waste material. This waste could be converted into biogas that would, it is believed, generate up to 40 per cent of the electricity needed by rural communities in these countries.

■ A great deal of this Brazilian sugar cane crop is waste material that could be used to make biofuels.

Biomass is more readily available and causes less pollution than **fossil fuels**. For example, biomass may contain one thirtieth the amount of sulphur and produce one fifth the amount of ash produced by some types of coal. Like fossil fuels, biomass produces carbon dioxide when it is burned. However, carbon dioxide is one of the raw materials plants use for growth through **photosynthesis**, so the amount of carbon dioxide produced when biomass is burned cannot be greater than the amount the plant took in when it was growing. In theory, therefore, as long as new biomass fuel is being grown at the same rate as it is being used, the carbon dioxide levels in the atmosphere should not be affected by biomass fuels.

■ Biogas digesters convert plant and animal waste into useful fuel.

Biofuel production

Scientists are looking for ways to produce economical liquid fuels from biomass. Biomass is the only practical source of renewable liquid fuel. Research has in the past focused on producing ethanol from corn. However, corn is expensive as it requires large amounts of energy, **fertilizers**, pesticides, and water to grow.

An alternative method is to use fast growing trees. Researchers try to identify the fastest-growing variety of tree in a region, so that it can be crossbred to produce a tree that grows even faster. Green wood can be converted into methanol which can be used directly in a suitable vehicle, or converted into high-**octane** gasoline. The only by-product is wood ash, which can be used as fertilizer.

ENERGY FROM SCRAPS

According to the US Department of Energy, biomass is currently supplying energy equivalent to well over a billion barrels of oil per year in the United States. Most of this energy comes from electricity generated by the burning of sawdust and wood scraps from lumber mills.

BIOMASS PLUS AND MINUS

Biomass fuel is bulky and difficult to transport. It takes about three tonnes of wood to produce the same energy as a tonne of coal. Even so, using biomass fuel to generate electricity is still practicable if the fuel is used close to where it is produced. In the pulp, paper, and timber industry in North America, for example, wood chips and paper scraps are burned to generate electricity for the factories that produce them.

■ Properly conserved, trees are a valuable and renewable source of energy and materials.

In rural parts of Asia, water buffalo manure is dried for heating and cooking fuel. **Biogas generators** in China produce methane, mostly from pig manure. Use of dung as fuel could decrease the amounts available for **fertilizer**, while growing plants for fuel would take nutrients from the soil.

Some environmentalists object to biomass crops because most would be monocultures – crops that are all of the same species. Monocultures are more vulnerable to attack by pests, which encourages the use of pesticides. Also, any region relying heavily on biomass fuels would be especially vulnerable if a natural disaster, such as a drought, deprived them not only of food but also of their energy supply. On the plus side, biomass crops can be grown on unused fields, generating much needed income for farmers.

Pollution control

In 1992 waste-to-energy combustor plants in the United States produced electricity equivalent to that generated by 30 million barrels of oil. This biomass is not as clean as wood, however. Pollution-control devices have to be fitted to combustor plants to prevent the release of harmful substances into the environment.

Biomass potential

There is no doubt that biomass has the potential to replace some of the **fossil fuels** now used to power smaller vehicles. It could also replace some of the fossil fuels that are burned to generate electricity. But these changes will not come about until vehicle fuel economy is greatly improved and more efficient gas **turbine** units become available for power production.

If the use of biomass was developed, it would lead to a reduction in carbon dioxide emissions. It has been estimated that if the countries of the developed world can achieve their biomass production potential, carbon dioxide emissions would be cut in half. However, this level of biomass use would require huge areas of land to grow the fuel.

ENERGY HARVEST

One of the biggest advantages of biomass is that it is renewable. The 30 years or so it takes to grow a mature tree is a lot less than the millions of years it takes for a coal seam to form. With careful management, it is possible to sustain a biomass crop by ensuring that the rate at which it is harvested does not exceed the rate of new growth.

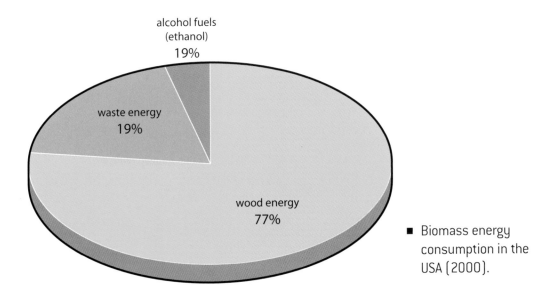

alcohol fuels (ethanol) 19%

waste energy 19%

wood energy 77%

■ Biomass energy consumption in the USA (2000).

"NOT IN MY BACKYARD"

There are no alternative sources of energy that do not have some impact on the environment. Take wind power for example. The wind itself is invisible, but a 60-metre (200-foot) tall wind **turbine** is difficult to avoid and few people want a wind farm as a next-door neighbour. The whirling rotors are also a danger to birds. A three-and-a-half-year study at Altamont Pass, a region of California where several large arrays of medium-sized turbines have been built, found that about a hundred birds of prey had been killed by the blades.

Hydroelectric horrors

There is no escaping the fact that dams drastically alter the **ecology** of nearby land and water habitats. Upstream from a dam, river life finds itself in what has become a lake and may have difficulties in adapting to the new conditions. Downstream, changes in the height, speed, and temperature of the flowing water can also have an adverse effect on river life.

Between 1950 and 1975 India lost 194,000 hectares (479,000 acres) of forest when waters were backed up behind new dams. In the Pacific Northwest of the United States, some dams block the annual migration routes of Pacific salmon, preventing them from reaching their spawning areas upstream. At least three species of salmon are listed as either endangered or threatened as a result of **hydroelectric** dam building.

■ Farming has been carried out on the banks of the Nile for thousands of years.

Hydroelectric dams can affect people, too, as the dams interfere with natural cycles of erosion and flooding. For example, along the River Nile in Egypt, annual floods had for centuries swept over nearby fields depositing a layer of sediment eroded from banks and plains upstream. Like all river sediment, it was rich in nutrients. After the Aswan High Dam blocked the Nile's flow in 1970, the seasonal floods came to a halt. As a result, the fields became less productive so that Egyptian farmers now have to spend more money on artificial **fertilizers**.

Geothermal drawbacks

There are definite drawbacks to **geothermal energy** as well. During the search for geothermal sources, roads may have to be built into wilderness areas, just as they do for oil exploration. Such construction work can disturb the local ecology. In Hawaii, for example, a geothermal development has destroyed parts of that area's last virgin tropical rainforest. The noise from construction work and from the operation of the geothermal plants can scare animals off.

Mineral-laden geothermal waters are disposed of after they are cooled. If they are emptied into lakes or streams they may harm water-dwelling organisms. The minerals in the waste water may also cause weedy growth to spread, clogging waterways and preventing oxygen from reaching the water. Hydrogen sulphide gas, which smells like rotten eggs, often rises from geothermal sites. Hydrogen sulphide can be oxidized to make sulphur dioxide, which may then combine with water in the air to form **acid rain**. Geothermal sites also release carbon dioxide, one of the **greenhouse gases**. However, this is much less than the amount emitted by a coal- or oil-fired power plant to produce the same amount of energy.

■ All geothermal power plants have an impact on the environment.

THE ALTERNATIVE FUTURE

There is no escaping the fact that we have become very energy demanding, surrounding ourselves with any number of power-hungry gadgets. Many people in developing countries aspire to own these items, too. A balance has to be found between consumption and production if there is to be a sustainable energy future. As well as technical solutions, social and political solutions will also have to be found. Can this be done?

In 1971, the world consumed the energy equivalent of 4,722 million tonnes of oil, 97 per cent of which was accounted for by **fossil fuels**. Twenty years later consumption was up to 7,074 million tonnes, 90 per cent of which was from fossil fuels, the 7 per cent drop having been taken up by nuclear power. By 2010, energy consumption is projected to rise to the equivalent of 11,500 million tonnes, with fossil fuels still accounting for 90 per cent.

The oil industry continues to discover new oil deposits by developing more effective methods of oil exploration. Improved technology allows oil to be taken from places that were previously inaccessible, such as deep-water sites. But this does not alter the fact that fossil fuels are a finite, nonrenewable resource that cannot meet the increasing demands for energy. Sustaining our energy usage may not be an issue for us today, but it will be for our not so distant descendants.

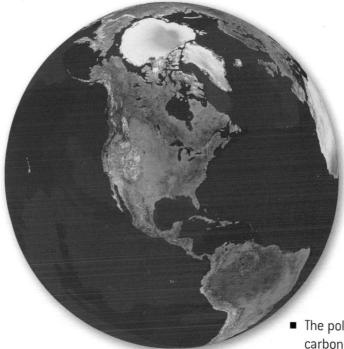

■ The polar icecaps are melting. Are carbon dioxide emissions to blame?

Energy and economics

The driving force behind practically all technological developments has been the desire to make money. This may seem cynical, but it is hard to deny. Car manufacturers, for example, will only make environmentally friendly cars if people want to buy them. The electric car was doomed because nobody wanted it. It was just too inconvenient to run. On the other hand, everyone can understand the benefits of fuel efficiency and getting more for your money and people will happily buy a car that goes further for less.

We will continue to rely on fossil fuels for our energy needs for as long as possible because there is nothing as cheap and efficient as coal, oil and gas. Sixty-four per cent of the world's electricity supply is generated by burning fossil fuels; 18 per cent comes from **hydroelectric** power, 17 per cent from nuclear power and less than one per cent from all the other sources discussed in this book, including **geothermal**, **biomass**, wind, tides, and solar power. Nuclear power is falling from favour and its use is expected to decline over the next few decades. So will solar power take its place? No, it will in all likelihood still be fossil fuels.

If we are to have a sustainable future we have to learn to value people over power. We have to stop looking for short-term gain and start thinking about the future – not just our own future, but the future for all those who come after us. Fortunately, there are some signs that we might just do that.

■ The hydroelectric power plant at Niagara Falls produces about 1950 megawatts of electricity.

SAVING FOR THE FUTURE

More and more companies in the industrialized nations are changing the way they heat and light their buildings, not only through a public-spirited desire to reduce **greenhouse gas** emissions, but also to reduce their energy bills. The reductions achieved often exceed those called for in the 1997 Kyoto Treaty, an international agreement on global warming. The Treaty's goal is to reduce greenhouse gas emissions by just over five per cent from their 1990 levels. However, the Treaty has been dealt a major blow by the fact that countries such as the USA and Australia have not ratified it, fearing that the targets set by Kyoto would damage their economies.

Companies are coming to realize that being environmentally sound can mean savings, not costs. Royal Dutch/Shell, for example, is aiming to reduce emissions of greenhouse gases at its plants to a projected five per cent below the levels of 1990 by 2010. Pharmaceutical giant DuPont aims to cut its greenhouse gas emissions by 65 per cent between 1990 and 2010. Boeing aircraft company upgraded its lighting and reduced its use of electricity for lighting by 90 per cent. This means in effect 100,000 tonnes less of carbon dioxide entering the atmosphere every year.

■ The Boeing aircraft company have made substantial
  savings by simply upgrading their lighting.

Developing needs

Many energy planners believe that if we are to meet world energy needs, we should consider the following aspects of all alternative energy sources.

- Their suitability to particular places. For example, Switzerland may have the potential for wind and **hydroelectric** power, but it would be pointless to try to transport energy from wave **generators** into the same country.

- Their environmental and health risks. Renewable sources don't release the kinds of air pollutants that burning fuels do, yet as we have seen they raise other environmental issues. A 100 per cent safe and reliable power source is probably an impossible dream but how close do we have to get to be happy to use it?

- Who will pay to research and develop the alternative energy sources? For example, some alternative energy sources may be useful mainly in developing nations where governments are unable to pay to develop them. Would it be in the interest of the governments of industrial nations to help pay for these, or should each country be expected to develop its own sources? Many developing countries have large coal resources. Should they not be allowed to develop them?

- How can the many different energy sources of the future be integrated into a global system that will make the best use of the strengths, and minimize the drawbacks, of each?

The price to pay

For many people, energy efficiency is only attractive if it is cost effective in the short term. They may ask, for example, "Is it cheaper to buy insulating material for the house or to buy extra fuel to heat it?" The question that has to be asked is this: "Is the short-term economic gain outweighed by a future environmental price?"

People, it seems, are not too good at taking the long-term view. There are few politicians, for example, who seem prepared to make unpopular, vote-losing decisions, such as introducing taxes on carbon fuels, or raising motor vehicle duties in order to cut back on carbon dioxide pollution. While insulating material might cost a little extra now, your grandchildren might be grateful that you didn't burn that extra fuel.

ALTERNATIVE ENERGY STATISTICS

HOW MUCH ENERGY IS ALTERNATIVE ENERGY?

(Figures are a percentage of the total energy use for Europe)

Hydroelectric

Pluses: well-established technology; large **hydroelectric** plants can generate a lot of power; no carbon dioxide emissions

Minuses: environmental damage caused by dam building; lack of suitable sites

2000: 13%   2010: 12.4% (estimate)

Wind

Pluses: technology is improving with individual machines capable of generating three megawatts being developed; no carbon dioxide emissions

Minuses: turbines are noisy and unsightly; lack of suitable sites; wind doesn't blow continually

2000: 0.2%   2010: 2.8% (estimate)

Photovoltaic/Solar

Pluses: completely renewable energy source; can be used anywhere; no carbon dioxide emission

Minuses: requires a large area to generate much power; technology is expensive (although prices are falling)

2000: 0.03%   2010: 0.1% (estimate)

Fuel cells

Pluses: could replace internal combustion engines as a power source for cars; no carbon dioxide emissions

Minuses: require fossil fuels to produce the hydrogen fuel; expensive technology at present

2000: 0%   2010: 0% (estimate)

Biomass

Pluses: plentiful sources in wastes from agriculture and forestry; a renewable fuel; established technology

Minuses: creates pollution, including carbon dioxide emissions; expensive to collect, transport and store biomass

2000: 0.95%   2010: 8% (estimate)

TOP 10 WIND ENERGY PRODUCERS

(in megawatts: 1 megawatt = 1 million watts)

Germany	16629
Spain	8263
USA	6740
Denmark	3117
India	2965
Italy	1125
Netherlands	1078
Japan	896
UK	888
China	764

(Source: World Wind Energy Association, figures for end 2004)

FIND OUT MORE

There's loads of information on the Internet and in books if you want to learn more about alternative energy sources. Use a search engine such as www.google.com to search for information. A search for the words "alternative energy" will bring back lots of results, but it may be difficult to find the information you want. Try refining your search to look for some of the people and things mentioned in this book, such as "wind energy" or "global warming".

More Books to Read

Graham, Ian. *Energy Forever: Water Power.* London: Hodder Wayland, 2001

Puay, Lim Cheng. *Green Alert: Our Warming Planet.* Oxford: Raintree, 2004

Saunders, Nigel and Steven Chapman. *Energy Essentials: Renewable Energy,* Oxford: Raintree, 2004

Websites

www.sciencemuseum.org.uk/exhibitions/energy
Discover loads of information and activities about different sources of energy.

www.bbc.co.uk/climate
Here you can find information about how the energy resources we burn affect our climate.

GLOSSARY

acid rain   rain that has been made acidic by the presence of sulphur dioxide from burning coal, and nitrogen oxides from car exhausts and other sources. These gases dissolve in the water vapour in the air, forming sulphuric and nitric acids.

atoms   smallest units of matter that can take part in a chemical reaction; the smallest parts of an element that can exist

biofuel   fuel that is derived from living material, such as wood

biogas   fuel, especially methane gas, produced by fermenting living material

biomass   biomass fuel is organic matter, such as wood and other plant materials and animal wastes, used as a fuel

boom   floating beam used to form a barrier over the surface of water

chemical energy   energy held in the bonds that hold atoms together in molecules. It is released during a chemical reaction.

consumer   someone who buys and uses goods or services

ecology   relationships between living things and their environment, and the study of these relationships

ecosystem   community of living organisms together with their non-living environment

electrolysis   separating elements of a fluid substance by passing an electric current through it

ethanol   another name for ethyl alcohol, which is found in alcoholic drinks.

fertilizer   chemical or natural substance added to soil to provide nutrients for plant growth

fossil fuels   fuels produced through the action of heat and pressure on the fossil remains of plants and animals that lived millions of years ago. The fossil fuels are coal, petroleum and natural gas.

fuel cell   device similar to a battery that converts chemical energy into electrical energy using hydrogen as a fuel

generator   machine that produces electrical energy from mechanical energy

geothermal energy   energy extracted from the hot rocks beneath the Earth's surface

global warming   rise in the average temperature of the Earth over recent years, which some blame on increasing levels of greenhouse gases, like carbon dioxide, in the atmosphere; others think it may be a natural climate change

gravity   force of attraction between any two objects

greenhouse gas   gas in the atmosphere, such as carbon dioxide or water vapour, that absorbs heat radiated from the Earth's surface that would otherwise escape into space

heat energy   energy associated with the motion of atoms and molecules

hybrid   something made by combining two different things and having some of the qualities of both

hydroelectric/hydroelectricity   relating to the production of electricity using the energy of flowing water to spin a turbine

insulate/insulation   something that prevents the passage of heat or electricity

internal combustion engine   engine in which the fuel is burned inside the engine

kinetic energy   energy of movement

micro-organisms   living things that are too small to be seen with the naked eye

molecule   two or more atoms joined together by chemical bonds; if the atoms are the same it is an element, if they are different it is a compound

natural gas   a mixture of methane and other gases found underground that can be used as fuel. Natural gas is a fossil fuel formed from the remains of once-living organisms.

nuclear energy   energy in the nucleus of an atom released when a large nucleus breaks down into two smaller nuclei (fission) or when two small nuclei combine to form a larger nucleus (fusion)

nuclear fusion   process by which two small atomic nuclei combine to produce a single larger nucleus with the release of a great deal of energy

octane   a measure of the properties of petroleum fuel

OPEC   Organization of Petroleum Exporting Countries, an inter-governmental organization that co-ordinates the petroleum policies of its member countries

oscillating   moving back and forth at a regular speed

petroleum   thick, yellowish-black liquid mixture of hydrocarbons found beneath the surface of the Earth. It is a fossil fuel formed by the action of bacteria, and the forces of high pressure and temperature, on the remains of marine plants and animals over millions of years.

photosynthesis   process by which green plants and some other organisms harness the energy of sunlight to make sugars from carbon dioxide and water

photovoltaic cell   device that converts light energy into electrical energy

potential energy   energy stored within a system as a consequence of its position or state

recycle   to convert waste into material that can be used again

renewable energy   energy from a source that can be restored; most such sources (wind, tides, waves) can be traced back to the energy of the Sun

silicon   chemical element with properties that make it invaluable to the electronics industry

solar energy   energy from the Sun

synthetic   describes something that has been made artificially

turbine   engine in which a fluid is used to spin a shaft by pushing on angled blades like those on a fan. Turbines are used to spin generators for producing electricity.

INDEX